Little Rhymes
for Young Minds

ORIGINAL POETRY BY
Fiona Mobbs

Personal Poet Fiona Publishing

Huff the Magic Dragon

Huff the Magic Dragon
Lived in Clacton-on-Sea.
He had many friends
With whom he would sup tea.

One day he had a problem
His huff ran out of puff!
And all he wanted to do
Was lounge round in the buff!

His friends were worried
They'd not seen Huff depressed.
They'd never known him not
Want to even get dressed!

They decided to rally round,
And bought cakes for ten pound.
They told jokes and made lots of tea,
Hoping he would again be happy.

But it was a lost cause –
Huff stayed behind closed doors.
Huff's twin even came to town
Hoping that would bring him round.

Then one day it all changed
Huff's puff he somehow regained.
We'll never know what happened
But Huff's spark has been reawakened.

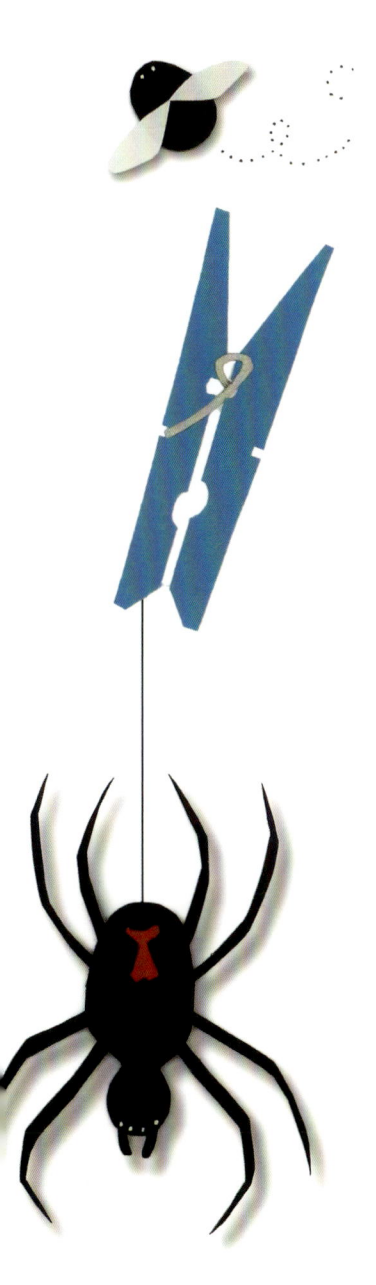

Eric the Spider and Derek the Fly

Eric, the spider, had eight long legs.
He loved to dangle from washing line pegs.
When anyone came to hang out clothes,
He would hide to protect his sensitive toes.

Eric, the spider, was black and hairy,
And liked to think he was mighty scary.
He realised his scariness wasn't a dream,
'Cos lots of people would run off and scream.

Derek was a formidable black fly –
He'd won cups for flying up high in the sky.
Fearless and skilful, were his signature things.
In the fly world he was "King of Kings".

Eric was dreaming of snaring a fly,
When Derek flew into the sight of his eye.
Little did he know what fate lay in wait
As Eric was thinking what could be on his plate.

But luckily Derek had a brilliant escape,
'Cos another fly slid in through the front gate,
And found his wings sticky with glue –
A special mixture from the spider's shoe!

So Derek lived for another day
And his friends all said "Hip, hip hooray!"
The moral of the story is always fly high
As you never know when a spider is nigh.

Timothy (the giant) Tuna

Timothy Tuna stood out amongst his peers
Maybe 'cos he'd had a few too many beers.
He hated being this big –
Even his brother called him a pig!

Timothy was hurt and upset
So he decided not to be a reject.
He swam off to find another home,
New friends and fishes that wouldn't moan.

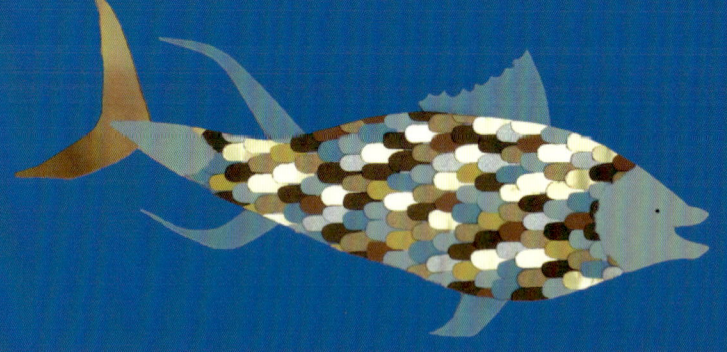

Along the way he met a shark
Nowhere to hide – even in the dark.
But Mr Shark didn't fancy a munch
As Timothy would be too big for his lunch.

Even the largest Minky Whales
On seeing Timothy turned on their tails.
Mr Stingray just had to snort:
"Blimey you're huge. Do you eat for sport?"

Finally Mr Octopus was kind.
He showed Timothy where he could find
A place to rest, a bed for the night,
Somewhere safe from his current plight.

In the morning it all became clear
Timothy needed Octopus's quiet ear.
Did he have friends, or family there,
Could Timothy be their protection "au pair"?

Octopus consulted his friends
And they all agreed
Timothy would be
A great catch indeed.

So there it was, tentacles linked
Timothy's new life was signed and inked.
With eight-legged friends who were equally freak
Against whom no-one dare speak.

The Seahorse

I'm a little seahorse,
Swimming in the sea.
I mind my own business
And nobody minds me.

I'm a little seahorse,
Swimming in the sea.
I encounter sharks and fish,
And see what they have
for tea.

I'm a little seahorse,
Swimming in the sea.
I see anemones
And plankton roaming free.

I'm a little seahorse,
Swimming in the sea.
I can speak and count:
One, two, three.

I'm a little seahorse,
Swimming in the sea.
I'm as happy as can be.
Lucky, lucky me.

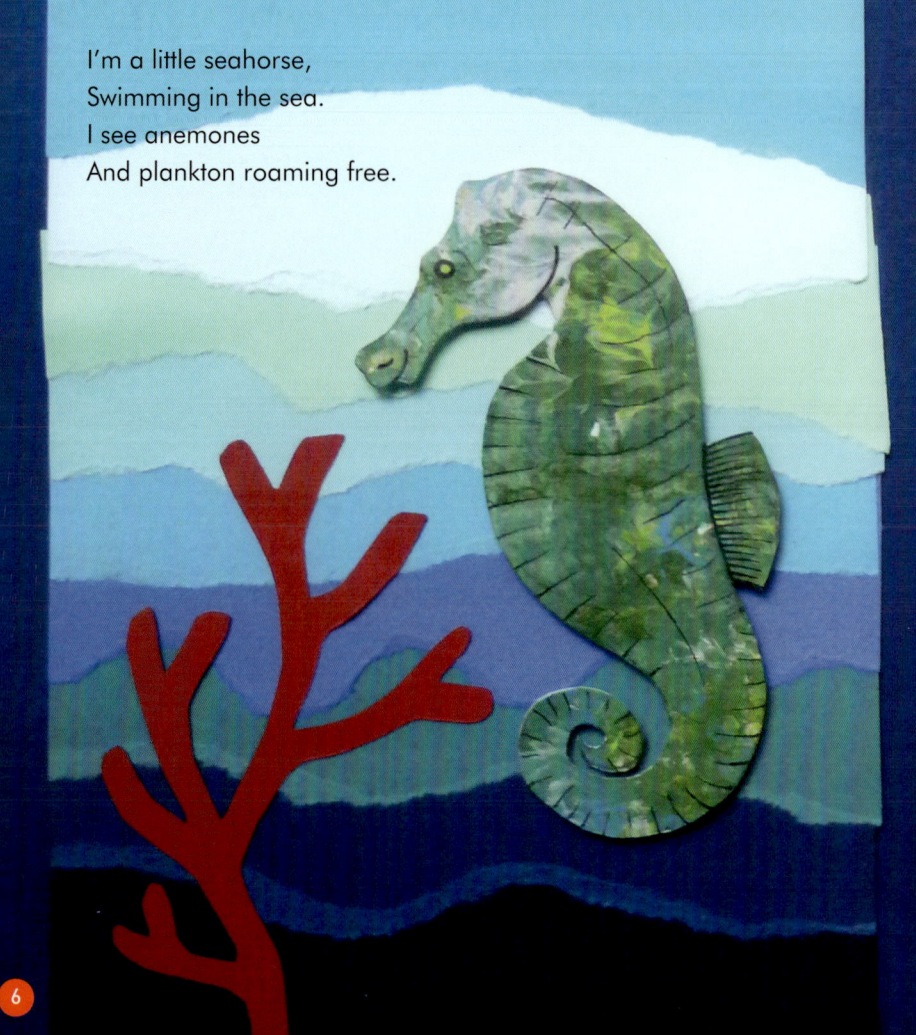

Sharkey's Tale

Sharkey was a fine white shark,
But he hadn't gained his "great"-ness mark.
So today was the day he wanted to count,
As he swum around St Michael's Mount.

He passed some boats that bobbed and swayed,
"That was my tail that made that wave!"
Sharkey grinned: I did well
It was me that made that awesome swell.

A shoal of cod swam quickly by
They didn't want to catch his eye!
But Sharkey was on a mission today
And didn't have time to stop and play.

He sniffed a human in the water
That's what he needed – something to slaughter!
He bared his teeth and raced on over
Only to find it was the shark catcher's daughter!

Better retreat quick as a flash -
Otherwise I'll be on their table with mash!
Maybe today's not the day to get my stripe –
There's always tomorrow – perhaps it's all too much hype.

The Gingerbread Man

The Gingerbread Man
Is a man who can!
He's accomplished and funny
And has a soft spot for honey!

He likes egg soldiers
And marmite on toast.
He's really clever,
But he doesn't boast.

He writes in ink,
And draws in chalk.
He has lots of friends,
Who also walk and talk.

He writes songs
And is musical
Playing many instruments
Both large and small.

If you see him
Give him a wave.
He also answers
To the name Dave.

Lucy, The Gingerbread Woman

The Gingerbread Woman is tall and slim,
And ties her hair with a rolling pin.
Her coat's too short, but that doesn't matter
She loves to stop and have a natter.

She likes baking cakes and things
And will try all manner of baking tins.
Her favourite cakes have jam inside
And marmite is what she can't abide!

She doesn't go far from home at all
And is well-known round the Village Hall.
But she's lonely and wants to find a mate
Someone who'll think her baking's great.

She tried dating on the Internet –
But it didn't bode well when one called her "pet"!
She's looking for someone who isn't a vet,
And will show her some proper respect.

Then she met a Ginger called Dave,
Who by all accounts was a people's fave.
He had lots of friends and was musical,
Playing many instruments – large and small.

They went out on a first date,
And each thought the other was great.
Dave asked Lucy on another date.
Have the Gingerbreads found their check-mate?

The Magic House

The magic house is painted pink,
But not a pink you'd naturally think.
Inside walls are green and cream
That magically help you sleep and dream.

Magic happens everywhere –
Whatever your wish will magically appear.
Fairies hide in this magic house
You might see them if you're quiet as a mouse.

If you're patient and really good
You might get a glimpse of a fairy's hood.
But beware – they don't like noise,
Especially from little girls and boys.

Hush now and go to sleep.
The fairies come out when you don't peep.
More fun tomorrow to come.
When you've had rest – today is done.

Twixt and Between

On the shelf I play all day,
Looking at you, as I hide away.
My name is Twixt and I live between
Things on the shelf that can be seen.

I gather dust to throw away
To save my owner moving things.
Then I fret less about being found
As I dance in my fun playground.

If you should notice me
When I'm out and about.
Please give me a little wink
So I don't get found out.

Dorothy's Red Shoes

Dorothy asked Toto
What she should do
When suddenly she discovered
She only had one shoe.

Scarecrow offered his old boots
But full of earth and roots
They didn't fit her small feet
And the outcome was not upbeat!

You'll never guess what happened next
(Well, thanks to Tin Man's text) –
Cinderella had a spare
Of right-sized pretty footwear!

Now Dorothy could click, click, click
Then was home super quick.
Now there's someone else you know,
Who loves shoes with a mandatory bow.

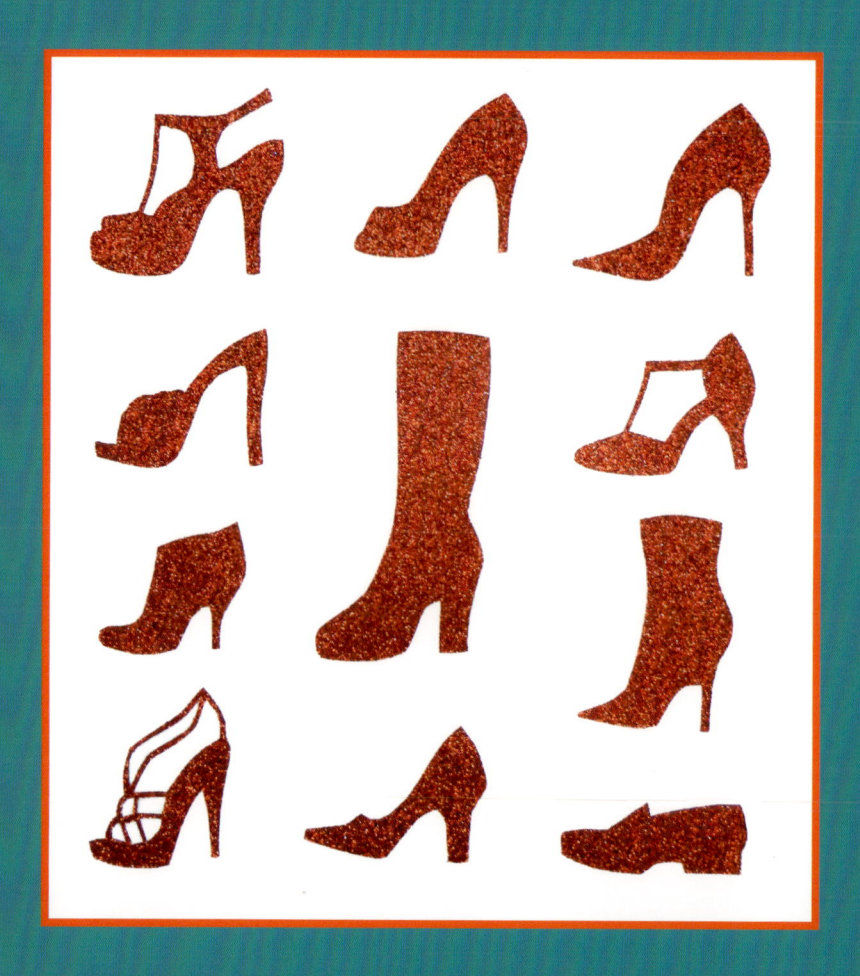

The Lonely Scarecrow

Life just happens to me,
As I stand here quite lonely.
Not even birds for company.
I must be so ugly.

But what's this? A possible friend?
She's just appeared down the end!
Do they know I'm lonely?
Have they heard my quiet plea?

No tatty hat on her head.
She looks the biz it has to be said!
Is that shoes with different heels?
Unlike mine with toe steels.

I hope this isn't my demise
I'm seeing with my own eyes.
So I decide I need to ask,
"What exactly is her task?"

The Faux Fur Ferret

I live in a cage,
And that's all right
'Cos I sleep a lot –
Both day and night.

When allowed out
It's all about play.
I have such fun
In every way.

Whilst I'm out
Manners are few.
'Cos I squeak and fart
Sadly a bit "beaucoup".

My adopters look after me,
Thanks a lot: you set me free.
They could've chosen another pet
Lots were on offer from the local vet.

Back in my cage, PJs on
Snuggling up and getting warm,
With my brothers, I'm so cute,
Settling down in my faux fur suit.

The Cat that Talks with Her Tail

When I awoke today
I was a bit scared.
What would the day bring?
And, was I prepared?

I met a cool cat
Who thought he could sing.
So I thought I would ask,
If he could teach me something.

Then I met another,
Who thought he could dance.
But all he could do
Was spin me to a trance!

The thing is,
I lost my voice –
Through an accident,
That wasn't by choice!

So as far as singing or dancing goes,
All I can do is display my toes.
But I do have a special talking tool
Which is fixed to my bottom and does it all!

I wave it fast when I'm happy and glad,
And puff it up when I'm frightened or sad.
So don't feel sorry for me
I count myself very lucky!

About the author

Fiona Mobbs MA, worked as a Human Resources professional for over 25 years in public and private enterprise. Dreaming of working for herself one day, she had the opportunity to leave paid employment and become a self-employed entrepreneur in 2013. Initially setting out in a totally different direction (although five years of training and preparation had taken place), this initiative soon gave way to another, which was rather more unplanned – becoming a personal poet!

Fiona had been writing rhymes about her business to use for a "one minute pitch" when networking, and some of the audience expressed their view that Fiona seemed to have a talent and urged her to do something about it. So, Fiona became "Personal Poet Fiona" – bespoking rhymes for any occasion. Quickly, commissions came in for other business one minute pitches, business Christmas cards, special birthday cards and speeches, wedding speeches, and rhymes for baby showers.

Fiona prefers to write short rhymes with comedy where possible. She does have a Facebook page, where you can see some of her other work, including some more serious poems (PersonalPoetFiona).

This is her first book, written for children. It is hoped that those aged 5 to 12 will appreciate these rhymes and wonderful illustrations (thanks to Hannah Bottomley). There are some challenging words on purpose, to hopefully extend a child's curiosity and development.

ENJOY!

Email feedback is welcome at fiona@personalpoetfiona.co.uk.